T0128683

ALPHABET ANIMALS

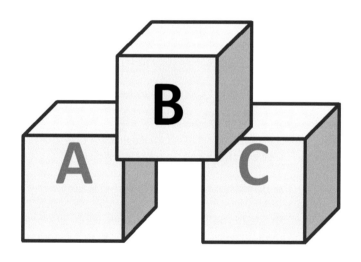

BY

"GRANDMA" GRACE BAKER

AuthorHouse™
1663 Liberty Drive
Bloomington, IN 47403
www.authorhouse.com
Phone: 1-800-839-8640

Published by AuthorHouse 03/22/2013

ISBN: 978-1-4817-3074-7 (sc)
978-1-4817-3156-0 (e)

Library of Congress Control Number: 2013904738

authorHOUSE®

Dedication:

I dedicate this book to my awesome sisters,

Audrey and Joyce. Thank you for your

unending love, support, and friendship

that you have always freely given.

Acknowledgement:

Grateful acknowledgement goes to my son,

Chuck, for his creative input. A big thanks

also goes to the rest of my family and

friends for their encouragement.

Alphabet Animals: Table of Contents

Ltr	Animal Type	Person's Name	Poem Title	
A	Ant	Audrey	Busy Little Ant	7
A	Antelope	Ashley	Awesome Antelope	7
B	Bee	Brian	Bee Buzz	8
B	Butterfly	Beth	Butterfly Dreams	8
C	Cat	Clifton	Cool Cat Rider	9
C	Crocodile	Carla	Rockin' Crocodile	9
D	Dog	Danny	High Flying Dog	10
D	Dolphin	Debbie	Dolphin Races	10
E	Eagle	Eva	Sky High Eagle	11
E	Elephant	Emma	Elephant Playday	11
F	Flamingo	Fatima	Flamingo's Ballet Recital	12
F	Frog	Frederick	Froggy Fun	12
G	Giraffe	Grace	Giraffe Games	13
G	Goose	Gina	Goose's Art Show	13
H	Hampster	Hailey	A Hampster's Day	14
H	Hummingbird	Heather	Hummingbird Dance Dreams	14
I	Iguana	Isaac	Iguana Vacation	15
I	Inchworm	Ines	The Incredible Inchworm	15
J	Jaguar	Jesse	Jaguar Baseball	16
J	Jellyfish	Joyce	The Jellyfish Prom	16
K	Kangaroo	Kris	A Kangaroo's NASCAR	17
K	Koala	Karen	Koala Lessons	17
L	Ladybug	Laurie	Ladybug Lullaby	18
L	Lamb	Lucas	Lamb's Special Wish	18
M	Monkey	Maggie	Monkey Around	19
M	Mouse	Mary	Miss Mouse's Tea Party	19

N	Narwhal	Nicky	Narwhal's Bedtime Story	20
N	Nightingale	Norma	The Nightingale Concert	20
O	Otter	Oliver	Otter Delight	21
O	Owl	Oscar	Little Owl Learns to Fly	21
P	Parrot	Patti	Parrot Rhyme Time	22
P	Penguin	Patrick	Penguin's Winter Wonderland	22
Q	Quail	Quincy	A Quail's Birthday	23
Q	Quoll	Quinn	Meet the Quoll	23
R	Rabbit	Ruth	Rabbit's Fashion Parade	24
R	Raccoon	Robin	Raccoon Gymnast	24
S	Starfish	Sandy	A Starfish Pool Party	25
S	Swan	Sarena	The Majestic Swan	25
T	Tiger	Taylor	Dr. Tiger to the Rescue	26
T	Turtle	Tim	Turtle's Trip to the Circus	26
U	Unicorn	Urvi	Unicorn Magic	27
U	Ursus	Uriah	Ursus Bear Family Picnic	27
V	Vampire Bat	Vince	Halloween Vampire Bat Style	28
V	Vulture	Vicky	The Vulture Chili Cook-off	28
W	Wolf	Walter	Camping with Grandpa Wolf	29
W	Woodchuck	Willie	Woodchuck's Pinewood Derby Car	29
X	Xiaosaurus	Xavier	A Xiaosaurus Adventure	30
X	X-Ray Fish	Xara	X-Ray Fish's Treasure Hunt	30
Y	Yak	Yuri	Yak's Football Triumph	31
Y	Yorkie	Yvonne	Captain Yorkie's Cloud Ships	31
Z	Zebra	Zeke	Detective Zebra's Mystery	32
Z	Zenaida Dove	Zoey	Secret Agent Zenaida Dove	32

Disclaimer: The names of all the animals are fictional and do not reflect an actual person.

BUSY LITTLE ANT

Once there was a baby ant
And Audrey was her name.
She wanted to grow up real fast
So she played a little game.

    She would find the tallest plant
    Then climb up, oh so high!
    Pretend she was a giant ant
    Who could reach up to the sky.

        Logs would magically be boats
        So a captain she would be.
        Some rocks became a mountain range
        Leading right up to a tree.

            Crawl up here and over there
            No time to waste, because
            There's much to do and much to see
            And adventures without pause!

AWESOME ANTELOPE

On top a densely wooded hill
I stand beside a slope
Of meadow grass all streaked with dew.
I'm Ashley Antelope.

    My home is on an open range
    Of land stretched far and wide.
    My friends are buffalo and deer
    Who roam the countryside.

        When I was just a little calf,
        My mom watched over me.
        Each year I grew till now I am
        All grown up finally.

            It's awesome just to run and leap,
            Find rainbows in the sky,
            Splash water in the nearby creek,
            Or watch the clouds roll by.

BEE BUZZ

From a bouncy baby bumblebee
I've grown much bigger finally.
My name is Brian Buzzworthy
And I'm a big bee now.

    In school, I've learned my ABC's
    And how to buzz a song on key
    But flying is my specialty
    I practice every day.

        To keep from falling off, you see,
        I must take care to land gently
        And flowers are especially
        A challenge when they sway.

            My cousin is a honey bee
            There's going to be a big party
            With bees from both our families
            And tons of fun allowed!

BUTTERFLY DREAMS

Out in a meadow near a small hill
A field full of flowers grew,
And under a lovely clear blue sky
Beth, the butterfly, flew.

    I love to dream of far off places
    And flowers help me pretend
    To visit countries, imagine sites,
    And enjoy the smells in the wind.

        Colored tulips take me to Holland
        With windmills and wooden shoes,
        Water lilies in a nearby pond
        Are any tropic I chose.

            There's Irish Moss and English Ivy,
            Dutch Clover, and Meadow Foam,
            Grecian Roses, and Chinese Lilac,
            Then daisies bring me back home.

COOL CAT RIDER

Clifton Cat strapped on his helmet
He was eager to start the day
'Cause he was taking a road trip
On the scenic coastal highway.

His motorcycle was ready
So he climbed on and started out
Riding on the road by the seaside
Soon spotting otters swimming out.

He passed through Big Sur's scenery
Of waterfalls and rugged cliffs
Along the way were lighthouses
With seagulls and seals and big ships.

He rode through a redwood forest
Seeing trees that grow tall and wide
Now the Golden Gate Bridge is next
And the end of an awesome ride.

ROCKIN' CROCODILE

My name is Carla Crocodile
You may have heard of me
'Cause I'm a famous teen rock star
With fans from sea to sea.

My concerts always sell out fast
This band's the best around
It's like a special holiday
When we come to your town.

We play the very latest hits
From blues, hip-hop, and rock
Soon everyone is grooving to
A beat that's smoking hot.

The Crocodile Song is popular
The kids all sing along
The Crocodile Rock's another one
Come on and join the song.

HIGH FLYING DOG

Danny Dog is a talented guy
He flies an airplane through the sky
Soaring above the earth below
Through fluffy clouds we see him go.

Releasing smoke that leaves a trail
Behind the little airplane's tail
Creates the lines for words and shapes
From all the twists and turns he makes.

Flying loops in the countryside
Is like a roller-coaster ride.
Diving down and swooping by
That's his way of saying "hi".

Over a lake and fields of hay
The ground looks like a big bouquet.
One final barrel roll is planned
Then he is coming in to land.

DOLPHIN RACES

What a delightful day for a race
Out in the ocean spray
Thought Debbie Dolphin when she woke
One clear and sunny day.

What's the first race going to be
I want to try them all
There's flipper flapping, tail walking,
And rolling like a ball.

High jumps are my favorite sport
I can do a real fast spin
The underwater obstacle course
Is a race I think I'll win.

Spout spitting is lots of fun and
Diving deep is an art
Now everyone is ready to go
So let the races start!

SKY HIGH EAGLE

It's just before dawn on a crisp spring morn
Eva Eagle prepares for the flight,
Attaching the basket to the balloon
And securing the tethers just right.

With a little twist, the burner comes on
And inflates the balloon till it's high.
We climb in the basket releasing our hold
Now we are soaring into the sky.

The ground starts to look like a patchwork quilt,
And the trees are beginning to shrink,
You can almost reach out to touch a cloud,
And the sky starts to show streaks of pink.

The sun peeks out along the horizon
As a beautiful rainbow appears.
It will soon be time to start our way down
So let's give Mother Nature three cheers!

ELEPHANT PLAY DAY

Emma is an elephant
Who loves to run and play
With all the other little ones
Each day's a special day.

Catch a ball and toss it back
Or flap your ears real fast
Then squirt some water in the air
Sure wish the fun would last.

Let's play tag and tug of war
See who can balance best
Then play a game of hide and seek
Before we take a rest.

Sadly it is time to stop
For just a while, but then
Tomorrow is another day
To do it all again!

FLAMINGO'S BALLET RECITAL

Fatima Flamingo stretched out her wings
Tied the ribbons on her ballet shoes,
Adjusted her tutu and flexed her legs,
Now just a hair ribbon is left to choose.

She practiced her warm ups at the barre
Doing pliés and all six positions.
Our ballet star is ready to shine
Recitals are annual traditions.

It starts with a graceful arabesque
Leading into some tippy-toe spins,
Then glissade in a spiral circle
Spinning out and returning back in.

Some pretty pirouettes are performed
With an elegance that looks like fun,
Leaping and swaying in harmony
A final curtsy – Bravo! Well done!

FROGGY FUN

From hop scotch games to hip hop flips,
I jump and jive and jog,
Sometimes I float and watch the clouds,
I'm known as Frederick Frog.

My friends come by each day to play,
And practice jumping high,
We play leap frog on lily pads,
Or catch the biggest fly.

The Friendly Frog is a hollow log,
Where we all come to sing,
Our favorite songs are "Ribbit Rock",
And "Big Green Frog, the King".

Some tadpoles frolic near the pier,
As day turns into night,
While dragonflies buzz overhead,
And lightning bugs shine bright.

GIRAFFE GAMES

My friends and I had fun today,
Thought Grace Giraffe while chewing hay,
We stacked some blocks and sticks up high,
And made an awesome fort nearby.

Then built a birdhouse painted blue
Designed to fit just one or two,
We found a kite stuck in a tree
And pulled until we set it free.

While playing basketball we heard
A cry for help from a baby bird,
So back in the nest we lifted him,
Then went for a nice refreshing swim.

I've done my chores and now proceed
To find a favorite book to read,
Or video games are also fun,
With milk and cookies when I'm done.

GOOSE'S ART SHOW

Gina Goose had to step back a bit
To look at the painted canvas there.
This was the final one to complete
To take to the art show at the fair.

She closed first one eye, then the other
Tilting her head to the left and right.
Is something missing or is it OK?
Are the colors too dark or too bright?

Maybe a rainbow would look real nice
Or some flowers or birds in the air.
I try to keep my work creative
Adding a touch of artistic flair.

I like it best the way it looks now
It's simple with graceful, flowing lines.
I'm ready to go enjoy the day
And find ideas for more designs.

A HAMPSTER'S DAY

"Fiddle dee dee, Fiddle dee day,"
Hailey, the hamster, was heard to say.
"I think it's time to have some fun."
So she hopped in her wheel and took a run.

Then she climbed through her tunnel
To the tower up high
And paused for a snack
While she gazed at the sky.

Now she fluffed up her bedding
Then scampered back down
Where she found a striped ball
And pushed it around.

Stopped in at the food bowl
Where cheeks were stuffed tight
And ready to sleep now
Curled up for the night.

HUMMINGBIRD DANCE DREAMS

Lights! Camera! Action! It's time
For Heather Hummingbird to shine
While dancing round the flowers bright
And sipping nectar morn to night.

The honeysuckle gently swings
To match the fluttering of wings;
A tango through the trumpet vine
Brings wondrous thoughts into my mind.

The bright red cardinal flower seems
Just right to practice dancing dreams
Of jazz and jive and quick step, too,
There're many others I can do.

The fuchsia takes a light ballet
Or waltzing near the end of day;
A dancing star I'll someday be,
Till then I'm happy to be me.

14

IGUANA VACATION

Out in the desert where the wind blows free
Lives Isaac Iguana with his family
Anxiously waiting for this time of year
Our vacation time is finally here!

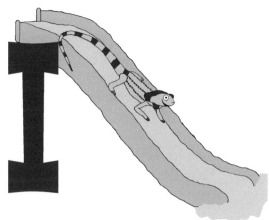

First, we escape to a water resort
With slides and a water volleyball court
There's a cool wave pool and tubing, too
Plus a waterfall I can swim right through.

A theme park's next and I can hardly wait
To ride the roller coasters and stay up late
I'll challenge my brother at the bumper cars
And an arcade game throwing rings over jars.

I'll eat some hot dogs and chocolate ice cream
See a scary show that will make me scream
Take a nice ride on a miniature train
Sure wish we could do this over again.

THE INCREDIBLE INCHWORM

Good morning, Ines Inchworm
You're so cute and small and gray.
I love to watch you walking
'Cause you move a special way.

Inch by inch you scoot about
Moving up to form a loop.
Forward now to straighten out
Gliding in a graceful swoop.

What are things you like to do?
Will you swing and laugh and play?
Maybe measure a leaf or two
Or just enjoy a sunny day.

Inchworm, inchworm on that tree
So incredible to see,
Will you stop and smile at me?
Oh, how happy you must be.

JAGUAR BASEBALL HERO

"What a wonderful, splendid day,"
Said Jesse Jaguar with a great big grin.
"It's perfect for the playoff game
And our team has the skill to win."

Expectations are in the air,
The players are ready to go,
"Play ball!" the umpire shouts real loud
Then here comes the opening throw.

First, we're ahead; then we're behind,
It's an exciting game to play.
The end is near and the game is tied,
Can the trophy be ours today?

I step up to bat; the pitch is thrown,
Hear the crack of the bat on the ball!
It's out of the park! The runs come in,
We win! We're the best of them all!

THE JELLYFISH PROM

There's lots of excitement all around,
Our annual prom is tonight,
My name is Joyce Jellyfish,
And I've got to look just right.

The Jellyfish Wiggle and the Twist
Are brand new dances to do,
You sway or twist from side to side,
Maybe throw in a jump or two.

The octopus who plays the drums
Is always awesome to hear,
Pink starfish hang from a seaweed tree
Like a lovely chandelier.

Everything looks so beautiful
With columns of bubbles bright,
And rainbow colors sparkle about,
Oh, what a magical sight!

A KANGAROO'S NASCAR

Excitement seemed to fill the air
As Kris Kangaroo got dressed,
Today's the biggest race this year
And I want to drive my best.

The stadium is full of fans,
The track is ready and soon
The All-Star Race will burst to life
On a perfect afternoon.

The sounds, the lights, the flags are all
A part of the speedway's spell,
So listen to those engines roar
And the squeal of tires as well.

Let's lift the hood, check one last time
Before we head to pit row,
The crew chief gives a thumbs up sign
And we are ready to go!

KOALA LESSONS

Karen Koala stood up tall
And asked the mirror on the wall,
When I grow up, what will I be?
A teacher just seems right to me.

I'd start each school day with a smile,
Review our ABC's a while.
Tell stories of our history
And look at some geography.

There's one more thing that we should do
Give each other a hug or two.
We've learned enough to make us wise
Now let's go get some exercise.

We'll climb up high into the trees
And munch on eucalyptus leaves.
Then snuggle in the branches deep
Relax, enjoy a little sleep.

LADYBUG LULLABY

Sweet little Laurie ladybug
Fly to the moon up in the sky
Gather some magic moonbeam dust
And sprinkle some nearby.

This lucky little ladybug
Went to the meadow near sundown
Danced with a leprechaun and then
A four leaf clover found.

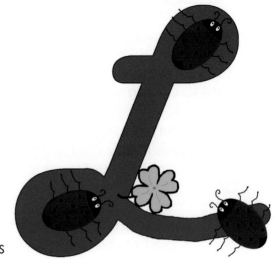

Enchanting little ladybug
Your touch both tickles and delights
You bring a smile to all who see
Your beauty during flights.

Come close dear little ladybug
Whisper a secret in my ear
Kiss the sunlit flowers of spring
Soon rainbows will appear.

LAMB'S SPECIAL WISH

Beautiful star up in the sky
I'm Lucas Lamb just stopping by
To gaze upon your beauty bright
And make a wish this special night.

I wish I may, I wish I might
Draw magic from your brilliant light;
Enough to pass around and share
To people living everywhere.

They'd find true kindness dwelling there
As well as love without compare.
And every time they pass it on,
It multiplies - it's never gone.

May hope spread like the rise of dawn
Throughout the world where we belong.
Then we'll all live in harmony
With a better future for you and me.

MONKEY AROUND

Climb up, climb down, climb all around
See Maggie, the monkey, swing
On hanging vines from tree to tree
As fast as she can spring.

So many faces can be made
With mouth and hands and eyes
And noises that are loud enough
To give you a surprise.

Go here, go there, go everywhere
Let's play some hide and seek
It's fun to jump and squeal and run
Along a clear blue creek.

And when it's time to have a snack
There's lots of fruit to eat
Like apples, oranges, and, of course,
Bananas are a treat.

MISS MOUSE'S TEA PARTY

Miss Mary Mouse has a lovely house
At the base of a large oak tree.
One sunny day in the month of May
She invited some friends for tea.

She baked some cookies with chocolate chips
And cupcakes with icing of white.
There were rice krispy treats cut very neat
And a punch that was sure to delight.

She filled paper cups with all kinds of nuts
Then tied a balloon to each seat.
Friends came for the fun exactly at one
And they all sat down ready to eat.

A wonderful day with laughter and play
Was greatly enjoyed by each guest.
With shouts of whoopee, they all quite agreed
Sharing tea with Miss Mouse is the best!

NARWHAL'S BEDTIME STORY

Nicky Narwhal got ready for bed
Under the ice in the Greenland Sea.
While his mother tucked him in, she said,
Here is a story that was told to me.

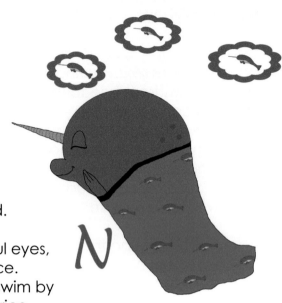

Once upon a time – long, long, ago
When the Intuits lived on this land,
At water's edge near a small ice floe,
A tall woman stood silently and planned.

She had long, dark hair and soulful eyes,
But her heart was as cold as the ice.
She watched the Beluga whales swim by
And wanted their magic at any price.

She tried to capture one of the whales,
Instead into the sea she was thrust,
Where she was changed into a narwhal
While her hair was twisted into a tusk.

THE NIGHTINGALE CONCERT

One little, two little feathered friends
Were sitting in a tree,
When Norma Nightingale stopped by
And then the birds were three.

As sunset splashes overhead
They all perch wing to wing,
These forest birds have come to spread
A special song of spring.

Tweet, tweet, woo-it, chew-chee, cheer-up,
Their notes are strong and clear,
Tweet, tweet, jug, jug, chew-chee, cheer-up,
So beautiful to hear.

At concert's end, they all take flight,
It's time for other things,
But they'll be back tomorrow night,
With more sweet songs to sing.

OTTER DELIGHT

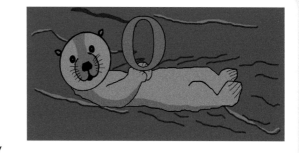

We'll have a delightful jubilee,
Thought Oliver Otter today,
When I'm the best swimmer in the sea
And win the first prize for relay.

My Backstroke practice feels just like play
When I watch the clouds way up high,
And later, with my friend, Manta Ray,
We will work on the Butterfly.

I could swim in Freestyle all day long,
It's like floating along on a breeze,
Every stroke helps make my muscles strong
While improving my expertise.

I'm very good at the Breaststroke, too,
Just gliding along like a swan,
So any swim style I'm asked to do
I am ready, so bring it on!

LITTLE OWL LEARNS TO FLY

Little Oscar Owl looked around one night
And wondered real hard with all of his might
Just what it would feel like when he could fly
Soaring and looping up into the sky.

My owlet brothers are bigger than me
And they're strong enough to fly from the tree.
I'm tired of always the one left behind
I'm going to learn but it just takes time.

I hopped on branches and stretched out my wings
I gathered my courage and tried some springs.
And to my delight, I fluttered onto
A much higher branch; Hoot – Hooray, I flew!

Now I'm happily flying everywhere
Through the moonlit skies and the clear, cool air.
What a wonderful feeling it is to fly
Winging way down low and then gliding high.

PARROT RHYME TIME

I can whistle, I can sing,
I repeat most everything.
Patti Parrot is my name,
Come play with me this rhyming game.

Pick a color and you'll see
It on a parrot just like me
Yellow, green, some blues and reds
On feathers, tails, and even heads.

Splashing in the water's fun
While underneath a nice warm sun.
Fluff my feathers till they're dry
Then fly up high towards the sky.

Rock left and right and up and down,
Swing back and forth and dance around,
I'll munch a treat, my wings I'll flap,
And then it's time to take a nap.

PENGUIN'S WINTER WONDERLAND

Patrick Penguin yelled with delight
While belly sliding on the ice.
Such an exciting thing to do
Because the speed feels really nice.

I'm going to build a snowman
But this time he'll look like me
With coal black eyes and curvy wings
And as round as he can be.

I'll join my friends for snowball tag
And go tubing down the hill.
Then ice skate for a little while
I've been working on that skill.

I'd like to go snowboarding now
And maybe race a friend or two.
Make snow angels and catch snowflakes
There's still so much I want to do.

A QUAIL'S BIRTHDAY

I've pushed real hard and pecked and scratched,
Look! There's a crack; oh, wow, I've hatched!
My mama checks me head to tail
Then says, "I'll name you Quincy Quail".

It sure feels good to stretch my legs,
I fall against some other eggs,
I see them hatching just like me,
And soon there'll be another three.

Our nest is cozy with us all,
I'm safe and warm though very small,
But I'll grow bigger every day,
And learn to fly and hunt and play.

Tomorrow we'll go hunt for seeds,
In bushes, grass, and even weeds,
I'll practice calls, my wings I'll flap,
Right now it's time to take a nap.

MEET THE QUOLL

I'm Quinn, a little cat-like quoll
As cute as cute can be.
And even though my name is strange
I'd like you to know me.

A quoll is a marsupial,
Australia is my home.
Through woods and rocky areas
Is where I like to roam.

I'm really small when I am born,
Stay in mom's pouch for months.
Then when I'm big and brave enough
Hunt bugs beneath tree trunks.

I like to stay up late at night,
My spots help me to hide.
Eat insects, nuts, some fruit, and grass
While having fun outside.

RABBIT'S FASHION PARADE

Ruth Rabbit looked through a dozen gowns
Picked one with a pretty white bow.
Add a white belt and colorful scarf
Then this one is ready to go.

My fashion parade is starting now
These new styles I'm eager to show.
This spring the colors are bright and bold
With accents that sparkle like snow.

We'll start the show with a lime green gown
Then a sunshine yellow and white.
Next show a flowing royal blue one
With rhinestones that sparkle so bright.

Here's a deep turquoise with silver lace
And a red one with streaks of gold.
A creamy white princess gown is last
A definite dream to behold.

RACCOON GYMNAST

I twist & turn while bouncing high,
Quite nimble and carefree,
I'm Robin Raccoon and someday
A gymnast I will be.

So many things I want to try
Like balance beam and rings,
Uneven bars are fast and fun
And vault needs good, high spring.

My somersaults and tumbling skills
Show growing evidence
That soon I will be ready to
Compete with confidence.

I study winners in this sport,
Take notes on what they do,
Then practice hard so one day soon
I'll be a winner, too!

A STARFISH POOL PARTY

Sandy Starfish hurried along
And met up with friends on their way
To a rocking party happening
In a tide pool at Half Moon Bay.

The seahorses will give us rides
Playing race games splashing around.
We'll bounce on orange colored sponges
And then dance till we all fall down.

Let's go through the limbo lineup
To see who can limbo the best.
Play hide and seek in the coral
And enter the surfing contest.

We'll build a sculpture with seashells
Use seaweed and sea urchins, too.
It will be a grand thing to see
Now there's still much more we can do.

THE MAJESTIC SWAN

On a tranquil day in the month of May
Sarena Swan swims by the shore.
The sun's just starting to rise in the sky
Shooting colors of pink, blue, and more.

I can hardly wait for practice to start
Cause synchronized swimming's a skill
Combining our learning with tons of fun
And making each day full of thrills.

We gracefully glide through a glistening mist,
Spread wings till the tips almost touch,
Form circles, spirals, and beautiful shapes,
Then stretch to the sky just so much.

Reflections of natural beauty and grace
Are displayed as long necks entwine.
A wonderful water world waiting for you,
So royal, majestic, and fine.

DR. TIGER TO THE RESCUE

Someone is running through the trees
Calling "Dr. Taylor Tiger, please
There's been an accident today,
We need you to come right away".

Down by the creek, we heard a yell,
A small puppy had slipped and fell,
His leg is caught under a rock
And soon he might slip into shock.

Dr. Tiger raced to the scene
And pushed a tree branch in between
The ground and rock then lifted up
To rescue the scared little pup.

The leg is wrapped; he'll be okay,
The tears and fears are soothed away,
How wonderful that help was near,
Let's give the doctor a rousing cheer!

TURTLE'S TRIP TO THE CIRCUS

Tim Turtle grinned from ear to ear
I'm super happy to be here
At the circus that's here in town
Spreading excitement all around.

The sideshow's quite a sight to see
The bearded lady frightened me.
A token gets your fortune told
That says your future will be bold.

I got a cotton candy treat
And in the Big Top, found a seat.
The clowns with monkeys make me laugh
That one's dressed up like a giraffe!

There's lions here and tigers there
And elephants with lots of flair.
The trapeze and the high wire acts
Are super awesome to the max!

UNICORN MAGIC

Once upon a time in a mythical land
Lives Urvi Unicorn where the sky meets the sand.
Mysteriously beautiful yet brave and strong,
Elegantly graceful with a horn that is long.

Every day is just perfect with skies so blue
That magic surrounds everything that you do.
Watch beautiful rainbows and butterflies flutter
Through fragrant flowers so colorful together.

At night the stars shine like diamonds that sparkle
So brightly you feel you've been touched by an angel.
Little crickets and frogs sing you sweet lullabies
While the lighting bugs circle and wink in your eyes.

Enchantment surrounds the unique unicorn
Through the marvelous legends passed down throughout time.
It's believed that to see one will bring you good luck
And a lifetime of happiness fully divine.

URSUS BEAR FAMILY PICNIC

In a lovely meadow in the woods
The Ursus bears are gathering near.
Uriah Ursus runs on ahead
To get to the family picnic here.

All the groups are arriving now
There are black bears as well as brown.
Even the big white polar bears
Have traveled the long journey down.

There'll be lots of honey sandwiches
And many other delicious treats.
I wonder who can catch the most fish
Or who has the biggest furry feet.

We'll enjoy a game of soccer
Play some tag or some hide and seek.
Maybe try a three-legged race
Gee, I wish this could last all week!

HALLOWEEN VAMPIRE BAT STYLE

As a shining moon rose in the sky
High over a large, dark cave,
Vince Vampire Bat opened up his eyes
And stretched his wings in a wave.

"It's Halloween!" he squealed in delight.
"My favorite night of the year."
And out he flew with everyone else
To enjoy some fun and cheer.

We'll fly in graceful, sweeping loops
Racing through the forest trees.
And catch about a million bugs
Floating in the autumn breeze.

Then back to the cave for a party
What a happy time we share.
My brother makes real funny faces
As our laughter fills the air.

THE VULTURE CHILI COOK-OFF

Chef Vicky Vulture took a big spoon,
Stirred the pot of chili again,
Then added a secret ingredient
To make it good enough to win.

This is the cook-off contest day,
Chefs arrive here from everywhere,
Though only the best get prizes,
We all bring dishes to share.

I love to cook all kinds of foods,
From soups to delicious desserts,
Experiment with pizza tastes
Or a sweet roll with filling that squirts.

A dash of this, a bit of that,
Then cook until it tastes just right,
I'm very good, I've won before,
Can I do it again tonight?

CAMPING WITH GRANDPA WOLF

Grandpa Wolf sat down on a log
With Walter Wolf right beside him,
Camping's always a special time
To play frisbee, relax, and swim.

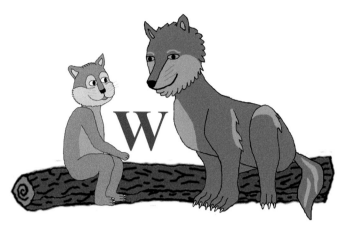

We start off the day with fishing,
It's exciting to catch a few,
Then paddle around the water
In a sturdy wooden canoe.

My brothers and sisters and I
Like to hike over nature trails,
Find lots of cool bugs and neat stuff,
And fly kites with really long tails.

At night we sit by the campfire,
Toasting marshmallows golden brown,
Telling stories of heroes and villains,
And watch fireflies blink all around.

WOODCHUCK'S PINEWOOD DERBY CAR

As he carefully opened up the box,
Willie Woodchuck's eyes opened wide.
Just look at that beautiful piece of wood
Plus more little pieces inside.

I shape the back with a little curve
And cut down the front nice and low.
So now the car has an angled shape
That will make the air quickly flow.

I may add an extra detail or two
And sand it until it's real smooth.
Then I'll paint it my favorite colors
Using yellow and green and blue.

Now I'll add on the wheels and the axles
Check to see if it needs some weight.
Then stick on some colorful decals
I'm ready for the starting gate.

A XIAOSAURUS ADVENTURE

I'm a xiaosaurus dinosaur,
Xavier is my name,
The day has finally arrived
"Let's go", my friends exclaim.

We walk along a jungle trail,
Adventure to pursue,
Strange plants and flowers greet our sight,
Large birds fly into view.

"Look over there on top that rock",
I pointed to my right,
A leaping lizard suns himself
As butterflies take flight.

We stop nearby a waterfall
To splash and rest a while,
Then off again because we are
Explorers full of style.

X-RAY FISH'S TREASURE HUNT

I'm going on a treasure hunt
I'm Xara, an x-ray fish.
To find a fabulous treasure
Is something I truly wish.

I'll explore tropical waters
Searching high, low, far, and wide.
And when there's something curious
Use my light to see inside.

I found a sunken treasure chest
And x-rayed it to see.
If something precious was inside
But it was quite empty.

There's beauty everywhere you look
Casting a magical spell.
These are real treasures worth seeing
You can see through me as well!

YAK'S FOOTBALL TRIUMPH

It's 4th down with 2 yards to go,
Yuri Yak calls play 24,
The football's snapped, the push begins,
A touchdown – and now we score!

The final game of the season
Is the most exciting of all,
And now the score is all tied up
So we've got to get that ball.

A win would mean a championship,
We just need another good run,
The football sails up in the air
The final play has begun.

We're close enough for a field goal,
A kick sends it soaring and then
The football drops through the goal posts,
Yak skill's given us the win!

CAPTAIN YORKIE'S CLOUD SHIPS

Yvonne Yorkie relaxed in the shade
Gazing up at a cool blue sky
Filled with clouds of all shapes and sizes
As they go drifting slowly by.

That one looks just like a small sail boat
Another like a pirate ship,
I could be captain on either one
Or take a cruiser for a trip.

There's one that could be a fast speedboat,
What fun to take it for a ride!
Or steer a Mississippi steamboat
With that great big wheel on the side.

I could make a dive on a submarine
Or take a fishing boat out to sea,
I could take a trip almost anywhere
What a wonderful time it would be!

DETECTIVE ZEBRA'S MYSTERY

I awoke one morning to a flash
And then heard a very loud crash,
Detective Zeke Zebra's on the case,
I'm ready to go in a dash.

  I step into the wooded site
  To find the cause of all this fright,
  I'm quiet as I blend right in,
  My stripes hide me out of sight.

    The rain last night has left wet ground
    But footprints just can not be found,
    I walk toward the area
    From where I had heard the sound.

      I see that lightning has struck that tree,
      The ground is littered with debris,
      There are limbs and branches scattered round,
      Success! I've solved the mystery!

SECRET AGENT ZENAIDA DOVE

Zoey, a smart zenaida dove,
Flies silently into the night.
Secret Agent Z26
Is on a special mission flight.

  A report of jewels missing
  Has everyone feeling alarmed.
  I want to find this jewel thief
  Before anyone becomes harmed.

    I fly along and soon I spot
    Some suspicious movement below.
    Swooping down for a closer look
    I can see it's the thief, I know.

      So I call in the location
      The police are there in a flash.
      They arrest this nasty burglar
      And the crime is solved just that fast.

Grandma Grace Baker is a grandmother to 3 wonderful grandkids. Her hobbies include reading, free-lance copyediting and writing children's poetry. Her poetic artistry has been published in twelve anthologies and she has won several awards including one from Great Poets Across America.

Another book you might enjoy is:

"Charlie Crab's Day at the Beach" by Grandma Grace Baker

Do you enjoy spending a day at the beach? So does Charlie Crab.

Charlie is going to spend today at the beach just relaxing, swimming, and enjoying time with his friends. However, special events occur with a starfish that gets stuck and some bullies. Charlie eagerly handles these challenges. His actions show that he is always willing to lend a hand (or rather a claw) where needed and that he won't tolerate bullying.

Printed in the United States
by Baker & Taylor Publisher Services